Game On!

Eddie Gibbons

THIRSTY BOOKS : EDINBURGH

© Eddie Gibbons 2006

First published 2006
reprinted 2009

Thirsty Books
is an imprint of
Argyll Publishing
Glendaruel
Argyll PA22 3AE
Scotland
www.argyllpublishing.com

The author has asserted his moral rights.

British Library Cataloguing-in-Publication Data.
A catalogue record for this book is available from the British Library.

ISBN 1 902831 98 5
ISBN 978 1 902831 98 5

Cover Illustration
Walter Molino

Printing
Bell & Bain Ltd, Glasgow

For my football first XI:

Brian Keeley
Bill Dann
Esther Green
Robbie Gibbons
Gerard Rochford
Birgit Weber
Peter Burnett
Gerry McElvogue
Brian Webster
and
Barbara & Jennifer
(for long sufferance)

YNWA

ACKNOWLEDGEMENTS

Thanks to the editors of *Storm Magazine* and the *Football Poets* website www.footballpoets.org where some of these poems first appeared.

A version of the poem *Look Away Now* appeared in *The Republic of Ted*, Thirsty Books, 2003.

AUTHOR'S NOTE

Some of the poems in this book were inspired by the writers listed below:

Page 14 Cargoes 2000 *John Masefield*

Page 16 Sonnet 15:00 *William Shakespeare*

Page 18 Assistance for the Linesman *Martha Collins*

Page 20 Tacit Tactics *e.e. cummings*

Page 22 The Long Game Closes *H. F. Chorley*

Page 23 We Millions Watching *Frank Scott*

Page 30 Royal, as in Real *Philip Larkin*

Page 41 Paris: Match *E. A. Robinson*

Page 46 Forensic *Joyce Sutphen*

CONTENTS

WE MILLIONS WATCHING

THE STARLIGHT CUP

Two coats are best for posts.
The bar defined by stars.
The ball, a small elusive
animal at twilight.

Two kids are best for this,
this game without a name;
this thrall, this all-consuming
spell of moonlight.

Hours are devoured.
Dark is the park.
In a blink the Sink estate
fades from view.

Sounds are muffled,
baffled in the lee of trees.
Only one stark bark
pierces through.

The Dream Team plays deep
into the night; no fright
will scare them aware,
shake their belief

that there's no relegation
from imagination –
nothing in the street can beat
this wakeful sleep.

The prize they win tonight
is theirs to keep.

FOOTBALL ASSOCIATIONS

Early inklings of crucial connections:
the bicycle pump, the casey adaptor,
the screw-in stud; all were somehow
connected with mud, the true element
of childhood, along with blood.
The pump connected to the ball.
The stud connected to the boot.
The boot connected with someone's head:
another little bleeder bled.

Saturdays were Matinees in Picture Houses:
Swizzles, Love Hearts, sugar-coated Disneys;
then out into the drizzle and the dash for a bus
to the playing fields, your kit wrapped in a towel.

Then, almost overnight, the game changed.
It was as if your brain had been rewired to
your trousers, all previous connections severed.

Lumps appeared everywhere,
especially in blouses.

All the houses
in your street became bordellos
of rioting hormones with nowhere to go.
I Am Curious Yellow was the show which you
hoped might have trailers of the vital action to follow:
the flirt, the kiss, the fumble on her parents' settee.
But especially the x-rated edits of carnal nights.

Hold your breath at the credits –
is your name up in lights?

FOOTBALL MATTERS

It mattered that some early-season Saturday
a Butcher's shop would close at twelve, and a factory
klaxon release a greased and grimed assembly line
to their bicycles, Lambrettas and Reliant Robins.

It mattered that the toast was buttered and the tea
was strong enough to stand a goalpost in, and that
the radiogram played *Orange Blossom Special* at full throttle
while the thick sliced cheese melted the bacon's heart.

Saturdays assembled around the working men
who hunched on Woodbined seats as football buses
wound along the threadbare streets of the far estates,
reeling the scarfed and rattle-roused spectators to the stadium.

Most bailed out at pubs along the thoroughfare: The Rocket,
The Sandon, The Cabbage Hall. Small boys sat on steps, cradling
bottled Stout, not daring to set foot inside to find their fathers
in the hubbub of the shouting Lounges, the shrieking Saloons.

When the jeaned and Brylcreemed masses left the overflowing
ashtrays and the dregs of Guinness glasses to the tender care
of barmaids, the pavements and the roadways streamed towards
the turnstiles and the choruses chiming on the nicotine breeze.

The press and cram of people made islands out of motorcars
and wrecked the privet hedges of the redbrick terraced houses.
A child's hand, held tight for fear of slipping from a father's grasp,
was securely gripped as any Captain's hold around a ribboned cup.

And this was the story and the match report for every game:
he held his father's hand and his father led him to the ground
where, sometimes on his shoulders, sometimes on the stanchions,
his father raised him up like a trophy, like a glory.

BOTTLE JOB

I was a toddler
when I first kicked
a ball – it was
a beauty – it flew
from my bootee
and knocked
my brother's bottle
out of his toothless
gob. Waving my bib,
I did a ruthless
streak past his cot,
then dribbled
his bottle around
the settee
and thought
this game's for me!

EVENT HORIZON

The stadium rose like a Starship
to meet us, floodlit as a Hollywood filmset.
We felt like extras in a Spielberg epic.

Unrehearsed, but eager for action,
we lifted, weightless, up fights of stairs,
drawn to the high illumined rim.

Stunned by sheer glamour,
we bathed in the glow,
swayed to the low cathedral chants.

The pitch was a dayglo tartan baize,
embossed with white geometries –
each corner flagged liked a landmark

in history; The Poles, Everest, The Sea
of Tranquility, where European evenings
brought lessons in geography, with banners

from Lyon, Dortmund, Bruges.
Familiar tunes with foreign words
cascaded in their cadences –

Forza Roma! Allez Les Rouges!

When the team captains met
in the circle the ref tossed a coin
that twirled in slow motion.

I wondered if somewhere out there in space
something familiar was taking place –
two teams, a ref, a ball, a coin. An arena
inside a spacecraft. A game between
Galacticos from opposing galaxies; aliens
feeling like extras on extra-terrestrial terraces.

CARGOES 2000

Wintergreen of Nivea, dubbin from Dior.
Flowing foam of Radox for bathing at full time.
With a locker full of Opium, Avon, Comptoir,
Lagerfeld, L'Oreal, and Calvin Klein.

Spicy scented Givenchy splashing on at Wembley.
Parking your Ferrari by exclusive stores,
With a chargecard for Demeter, Erreuno, Alchimie,
Trussardi, and Benetton, and Haute Couture.

Freezing cold supporters holding touted tickets
Bustling through the turnstile when it's raining stones,
In their outfits of cut price, marked down, Nike-ticked
Shell Suits, Reeboks and mobile phones.

PERFECT PITCH

In the deep mid-season winter
frost encrusted turnstiles click
like glaciers about to crack.

We coast between metallic clacks and enter
to discover a perfect pitch and not the rink
predicted by miles of icy pavements.

An abandonment would feel
like a form of bereavement
but the under-soil heating has kept

the game alive, and, we hope, kicking.
The singing starts in small scattered
choirs, fog-bound by their breathing.

Another sum exceeds its parts –
the voices swell in fits and starts to render
O Come All Ye Faithful pitch perfect.

SONNET 15:00

Should I support you on a Saturday?
You are too slovenly, too tardy, mate.
Rough hands will take that darling Cup of May.
They won't be yours, so just forget that date.
Sometimes you caught the eye of Eriksson,
but often is his team selection dim;
for every Gerrard there's an Anderton:
some sick-note who should spend time in the gym.
You get eternal summer breaks, all paid,
yet lose possession quicker than Biscan.
But still you brag about the time you played
in Italy for Juve and Milan.
So long as I can breathe you won't see me
turn up to watch you, Saturday at three.

RITUAL

Some run on the pitch
for their first kick,
others touch the grass,
lift the hand to their mouths,
kiss a finger, bless
themselves, and this
is a sacrament, a wish
for assistance to assess
the flight of the toss,
the height of the pass,
the weight of the cross.

ASSISTANCE FOR THE LINESMAN

First, you make a pitch and net inspection,
then you make a bee-line for the touchline.
Never cross the halfway line – it's not your jurisdiction.

Toe the line. Hoe the line.
Know the line between a dive and an obstruction.
See if the last line of defence can hold the line.

There's a fine line between the offside and the on.
So stay in line with play, make your decision.

Raise your flag to the ref in confirmation.
There's no time for a blink or hesitation.
Don't pussy-foot about, show conviction.
In your view and his align there's no remission.

The Stewards will be there for your protection
against an irate player's protestation.
The crowd will bay for your humiliation.
Beware of flying coins with sharp serrations.

You're in the line of fire, you'll be maligned.
Your lineage will be called into question
by fifty thousand fans and Desmond Lynam.

Stick to your guns, be persistent.
Most of all you have to be consistent.
Like me when I refuse to refer
to you as the referee's assistant.

A BOOKING FOR THE REFEREE

You've been booked for the big one –
Cup Final, the Millennium.

Smooth the silk of your kit with your palm,
test the whistle's shrill alarm.

What's this – shinpads? Well you never know
if some mad fool will have a go.

Tuck the notebook in your pocket.
Put your money in the locker. Lock it.

Look in the mirror at your poker face stare –
you're no Collina but you're no wilting flower.

You're the Law, the Judge, the Man in the Middle.
Whoever wins, you'll get your medal.

Check your watch, wind it up –
like you did to that player in the FA Cup.

Third Round, Prenton Park, you came down hard –
drew a flush of reds and said : pick a card, any card.

TACIT TACTICS

Here is the A plan: we play four-four-two,
with half-backs cutting in from either wing.
Two centre backs routinely clearing
to midfield men who play the forwards through.
Here is the main man: the ref's lips will blow
when wayward sinners wildly lunge, and bring
(unless requested for the quickly-taken sting)
the wall to ten paces reluctantly and slow.

This is the B plan: extra time will glean
a golden goal to bring the scorer fame,
as other days when foreign names were sung.
The match is on a knife edge, and among
slow deep defenders, stealthy and unseen,
some silver-booted striker steals the game.

LOSING STREAK

A naked man is running onto the pitch
followed by ten Stewards and one policeman.

We can't allow this! He must be stopped!
The naked man is wrestled to the ground.

Hooray, we cry, *hooray!*

The naked man is handcuffed and frogmarched.
The policeman holds his helmet over his helmet.

A naked woman runs onto the pitch: we ask
if she has some friends who'd like to join her.

THE LONG GAME CLOSES

No punts over the top, we've done with sweeping.
Instead, a slow build-up through midfield creeping.

We pass out to the flanks, the winger crosses.
Strikers nod their thanks. The long game closes.

We contemplate the worth of this endeavour –
the pass, the run, the swerve, the bullet header.

Results our team achieves – all wins, no losses,
the grateful crowd receives. The long game closes.

The floodlights flicker dim, the fans walk slowly.
A psalm, a prayer, a hymn's sung to our goalie

for rolling out the ball, not clearing houses.
The graceful moves enthrall. The long game closes.

WE MILLIONS WATCHING

This game is dearest to our hearts.
Through summer sun and winter rain
we millions watching play our part.
So hopeful at each season's start,
we fall, stand up, renew again.
We millions watching play our part.
When true companionship pertains,
no war nor strife shall break the chain.
We millions watching play our part.
When moral frailties depart
may peace and fellowship remain.
We millions watching play our part.
The groupings on the World Cup chart
bring nations to the new campaign.
We millions watching play our part.
Supporting is a noble art
when sportsmanship defeats disdain.
This game is dearest to our hearts.
We millions watching play our part.

A BRIEF HISTORY OF HALF TIME

HALF TIME HAIKUS

nil nil at the break
each team missed a penalty
empty nets both ends

ten thousand lighters
pass their flames to cigarettes
a terrace inhales

pie and bovril time
volcanic temperatures
scald our lips and tongues

the trannie's whisper
translates into whoops and shouts
rivals are losing

toilets overflow
bursting punters face the wall
thirty waterfalls

zipped up trousers turn
scampering towards their seats
teams take to the pitch

BRAGGING RIGHTS

Here is the difference between us and you:
one's number one, the other is two.
One wins so many, the other so few.

Our trophy room is packed to the rafters.
Your trophy room, with hollow laughter.
That's how it will be now and hereafter.

No-one can take this pleasure from me.
We're champions, champions, champ-at-the-bit-ions,
Champions of such high pedigree.

You're in the gutter. I'm watching our stars.
We polish silverware. You polish our cars.
Were Europe's finest footballing Czars.

You score against us. We hit you with three.
I wouldn't watch your team if tickets were free.
We're the crème de la Prem, you have to agree.

HICKORY DICKORY.doc

Hickory dickory dock,
West Ham ran down the clock.
When they scored one
a sub ran on –
no stoppage time was docked.

*

Tofik Bakhramov,
who some say let England off
in '66 v Germany,
was always welcome in Barlinnie.

*

Ally MacLeod,
Scots and proud,
led his team to World Cup glory,
or so it said on Jackanory.

*

Terry Butcher
required a suture,
like many folk in foreign squares
hit by England's flying chairs.

*

David Beckham,
England captain,
Plays in Spain
(It's no Brain Drain).

*

Bergkamp, Neeskens, Rensenbrink,
could score a goal before you blink.
But would those classy Cloggie chaps
admit to wearing ten Dutch Caps?

ROYAL, AS IN REAL

Royal, as in Real:
an intake of breath.
Then thousands exhale –
victors at the death.

Real, as in Madrid:
pageant and procession.
The Spanish power grid –
eternal possession.

With each olé approved,
they pass, run into space
for that slow-building move
played at Zizou's pace.

PREMIERSHIP PUNCTUATION

*| = hit the post.

o*o = a clash of heads.

^ ^ ^ ^ = waterlogged pitch.

"o" = through the keeper's hands.

/o\ = through the keeper's legs.

<>= midfield diamond.

+ = cross.

\+/ = high cross.

] = high wind.

( ) = who ate all the pies?

)(= winded.

% = 50-50 ball.

£££% = agent.

/o/ = through the channel.

(o) = in the hole.

(&&) = safe pair of (h)ands.

v = suggestion to the Referee

<o> = missed!

\o/ = goal!

#)))o = burst the net

|o = it was over the line.

o| = it was never over the line.

>>o = two-footed tackle.

<|> = keeper had nothing to do.

++++ = four-man wall.

^ ^ ^ ^ = the seagulls that follow the trawler.

YOUR POEMS

This poem is abowt
your Boltons,
your Aberdeens,
your Celtics &
your Cardiffs.

But it's not about
your Rangerses,
your Wolveses,
your Heartses or
your Hamilton Academicalses.

It's not one of your Novels or your Plays –
it's one of your Poems.

Stand up if you hate this poem.
But if you like it, please enquire about the author –
Who Are Ya? Who Are Ya?
Are you McGonagall in disguise?

He will be flattered by your interest.

You might have a pop at the poem
if you think you're hard enough,
but it's always handbags at ten paces,
and you only win when you're singing.

The poem will have been disappointed with that last line.

But it knows the First Leg is a half of two games.
It's taking each verse as it comes. It will go down to the wire
where the Fat Lady sings of parrots and moons.

The poem was unsighted for that spelling error in the first line,
but think twice before giving it the elbow – this baby's got
bouncebackability – it will bite your leg off, hit you with
the soggy end and sell you a dummy, you dummy.

But at the end of the day if it kept you away from
those stupid pundits then the poem done good.

FOOTBALL CHAIRMAN

Feeling like a goalie
under fire from all sides,
I ducked and dived, bobbed and weaved
to guard a spare chair for you
at the Old Firm game in the pub.

I even wiped the beer spills,
the Pork Scratchings (from itchy pigs?)
and unspeakable bits of pie from the chair.

When you arrived ten minutes after kick off,
I didn't growl through the sea of angry faces.

No, I grinned like
my nickname was now *The Cat*,

knowing that against all odds
I'd saved the chair –
kept a clean seat.

CITY v UNITED

How strange for Neville, Giggs & co.,
accustomed to the Cockney End
of prawn & lettuce Julians,
to play a game in Manchester
surrounded by Mancunians.

ON THE GREEN TRAIN

I got on at Montrose
and sat next to the Pope
and his wife, who were
on vacation from the Vatican
(they always travelled Virgin.)

They were short on conversation
but were polite in a Teutonic sort of way.

He polished his lederhosen Hot Pants
while she polished off the After Lent Mints.

He asked if I liked his Reservoir Bhoys
T-shirt, which I did.

Kyrie eleison! Johnny Hartson!
he muttered mysteriously,
then: *Boruc, Marshall, McGovern – The Goalie Trinity,*
and: *McGeady crosses better than me!*

He seemed to find this amusing
and he chuckled to Dundee.

As they alighted at St. Andrews
for a spot of golf he blessed me twice
for sneezing.

Then a Rangers fan got on:

*Haw, you, wiz that the Pape
I jist passed on thu platform?*
he enquired.

That is a correct assumption,
I replied.

Bloody strange things, trains! he said.

I nodded in confirmation.

ON THE BLUE BUS

I got on at Govan
and sat next to Ian Paisley and his wife,
who were on a fortnight's Shouting Holiday.

He was big on conversation
and very polite in an aggressive sort of way.

She was having 'Woman Troubles' and sat quietly
decommissioning her knitting needles.

Then Mr. Paisley's conversation
took on a familiar pattern –

Which team do you follow, follow,
and did your father wear the sash?

When I sashayed around the question
he muttered mysteriously –

Glory, Glory! David Murray!
then: *Oranges are the only fruit!*
and: *Can you play the flute, boy, play the flute?*

We were joined by the Inspector,
another Ibrox shouter,
and they got on like a barricade on fire.

They argued for the old 4-4-2
against the current 3-5-2,
and denounced the reformation.

Aghast at this faux pas, and, seeing many scarves
from the foe, Parkhead, the Inspector let him off
at Renfrew Cross.

Then a Celtic fan stood up:
Hey, wee big man, was that Paisley there?

No, I replied, *still two stops to go.*

ENGLISH FOR FOREIGN FOOTBALLERS

Sign
Sign
DOSH!
Cigar
Cigar
Golfclub.

Hack
Hack
FOUL!
Card
Card
Bathtub.

Pass
Pass
GOAL!
Lager
Lager
Nightclub.

THE SCORE

Having missed a score of chances,
the goal the scorer thought he'd scored
was scratched off the scoresheet for offside,

so the scoreline remained scoreless.
A win would have secured the club –
their name inscribed on the cup.

Instead, they had a score to settle
with the referee, who manifestly
had not scored for seasons.

As if to underscore the sore
feelings (the goal was a scorcher)
the forward fuelled the discord

by his scurrilous retorts to the linesman –
his scorching invective pouring scorn
on the poor man's decisions.

Perilously close to physical assault,
Security provided his sour encore –
he was summarily escorted from the pitch.

His manager's shrug offered little succour –
he'd been in the game long enough
to known the score.

POSH SPICE TAKES IT UP THE CHARTS

The cruellest chant of all
is saved for someone
who never kicked a ball.

Some would say of this song:
*fifty thousand Scousers
cannot all be wrong.*

But the girl is just a singer,
a wife, a mother,
a proud father's daughter

who's topped the charts,
got her hits out for the boys
and broke a thousand hearts.

Her *David wears my knickers* gaffe
spiced up all the tabloids
and gave us all a laugh,

so she should not be abused.
Chant this to that chanteuse:
Victoria, we are most amused!

PARIS:MATCH

Liverpool v Newcastle 31.08.97 (postponed)

Where's everyone today?
    The ground is shut and still.
There's no-one here to play.

The news from far away
    blows bleak and loud and shrill:
Diana's passed away.

We hear to our dismay
    the match is off the bill.
There's no-one here to play.

Why is it then we stay
    around the Anfield chill?
Diana's passed away.

Nobody kneels to pray
    though all have time to kill.
There's no-one here to play.

We wait for light's decay
    then traipse down Walton Hill.
There's no-one here to play.

We'd best be on our way.

THE SWEET SILVER SONG

THE ALAVES BADGE

I took the smile
you wore for me
in the bright café,
your words slipping
easily from tongue
to tongue, translating
my native to your native,
and I left you only silence.

Later,
I saw you in the square,
your black hair electric
in the glinting sunlight.
I heard your singing
echoing down Silberstrasse.

Later still, at the stadium,
as the time we had left became
unexpectedly extra,
I, fearful of a curse, unclipped
the badge you gave to me
and threw it to the ground.

Forgive me, Senorita.
It was my only hope.

Liverpool 5 – 4 Alaves (after extra time)
UEFA Cup Final, Dortmund, May 2001

FORENSIC

What happened here today
will melt into mythology,
and in the melancholy air
of some misty Saturday,
the whistle now blowing
will come to symbolise
something precious lost.

There will be a demotion
of hopes; folklore and old
songs will be sewn together,
sung and told forever as
distant recollections,
grains of consolation
for the dark days ahead.

See, someone will say,
it's almost visible:
the scuff of grass
where he placed the ball –
the brief union
of boot and history,
shooting into immortality.

A TILT AT THE TITLE

When Jamie runs,
Robbie runs, and when Steven
runs some stay behind,
drop off, track back, hold
the line, while others
hover at the centre, one foot
in either half, poised
perfectly between onslaught
and defence, as if a single scintilla
of motion would tilt the pitch
and the ball would roll unhindered
to nestle in the tousled nets.

THE OWEN GOAL

The one against Argentina,
set me thinking of my father
(some thirty years after)
slicing corned beef
for our half-time hamper:
sandwiches, crisps,
a bottle of Tizer.

I think of him cutting
the bread on the platter.
I think of the knife
cutting through butter.

ALL ALONG THE WATCHTOWER

It was always *The Watchtower* and *Awake!*
that my Mother, in her ecumenical muddle,
forced me to read every Friday night.
I went to bed shaking with fright.

She was hedging my bets against the Void.
Believing in everything, she had me circumcised
twice – once as a Catholic and once as a Jew
(so I would not go gentile into that good night?)

The things I suffered for her beliefs!
At least I kept the skin of my teeth.

Despite my protestations, she was hell-bent
on my salvation. I drummed beneath the banner
of the Protestant Boys of the Orange Order,
all of whom came to my Bar Mitzvah.

I had to walk from Huyton to Oxton
to find a Kosher chippy: six penneth of cloven
and a dollop of cud. But a single scoop of penicillin
soup made my poor stomach loop the loop.

By thirteen I was a Holy Wino, robbing my older
brother's Giro for cash to put in the collection plate.
I called every saint *mate*, and coveted their daughters
at Evening Mass, which I christened *Last Orders*.

By Jove! I learned the Jewish Quabala,
the Talmud, Koran and Upanishads.
I quoted the verses of the Rig Veda,
said Grace before I ate my supper.

Then one day I discovered
the word *Atheist*.
That's for me, too! I thought.
So I kicked into touch Buddha
and Shiva: bought a ticket to Anfield.
Now I'm a believer. . .

NIP AND TUCK

Then there was the bloke
on the radio phone in –

See that Stevie Gerrard,
he's magic, he is.

He's really nippy
for a midfielder,
and do you know what?

If I caught him in bed
with me missus,
I'd tuck him in.

CEREAL

The chant was offensive,
the play was defensive,
when the black winger
shrugged off
the Coco Pops jibe,
made a monkey
of the full back,
hit a banana shot
that snapped
crackled
and popped
from his boot,
spooned the brown ball
into the white net,
and turned,
one black hand
raised, to milk
the applause.

The white-hot,
red-faced
applause.

*(for Albert Johanneson,
Leeds United, 1960-69)*

REFLECTION ON DALGLISH

Cheering at the Kop end with my mates,
he appeared, as in that dream –
I was him and he was me.
After we swapped shirts both of us were drained
following a thrilling game. On scoring the winner
he stood, arms raised, right in front of me.
I pondered on the joy that he must feel,
giving so much to so many. With his quiet genius
he sent a roar of wonder through the crowd.
We were always enthralled,
watching his dazzling skills.
We came to see him play
game after game,
game after game
we came to see him play.
Watching his dazzling skills,
we were always enthralled.
He sent a roar of wonder through the crowd
with his quiet genius, giving so much to so many.
I pondered on the joy that he must feel.
He stood, arms raised, right in front of me
on scoring the winner. Following a thrilling game,
both of us were drained. After we swapped shirts
I was him and he was me.
He appeared, as in that dream –
cheering at the Kop end with my mates.

IRONY IN THE SOL

In a friendly held at Wembley,
as Cameroon run out,
mindless terrace racists shout
Get out of my country!

In a final held at Wembley,
when Sol gets in his swing,
mindless terrace racists sing
Abide with me.

THE VIRGIN AND THE GOALIE

He tipped her
over the bar
at a night club –

Keep the change, luv.

He ordered a highball, no ice,
due to his fear of slippery surfaces.

He was on the rebound, he said,
another long shot
had slipped through his fingers.

He had some extra time
to kill, so how would she fancy
being cradled in a safe pair of hands?

He thought he'd trapped her
but she back-heeled him
for a more striking partner.

He was too forward, she said,
and she didn't want to be handled
by someone out of his box.

He drank his Bitter,
swallowed his pride
and hit the streets.

She moved the goalposts.
He kept clean sheets.

v DOLOROSA

Fourteen stationed for the cross:

It was never a free kick! This ponce
of a referee is on auto pilot –
the defender is innocent as a lamb chop.

This lot use Klinsmann as their roll model.
Their forwards dive deeper than Galilee
But this one's riding on my shoulders.

A whistle at last!
He pushed me to the ground!
What, no yellow card?

The wall has got to move back.
While we're waiting I'll give
a quick wave to my Mum in the stands.

He's on my back again!
Ha, ha, Simo's just digged him in the ribs!
Now he's dragging him off me.

What the. . . ? Some girl has just rushed
from the crowd to wipe the mud off my forehead.
She was wearing a T-Shirt with my face on it!

I'm knackered. Thank God it's near the end
of the season. That winger's been skinning
me all game. Now the crowd's on my back!

But there's that girl, smiling from the front row.
She's got a couple of kids with her. A single Mum,
probably. She shouldn't have run onto the pitch.

Look, John, mark Matthew and I'll take care
of that centre forward. I owe him – he's had me
on my backside three times today.

They said we'd have a mountain to climb
to win this one. For crying out loud!
I've just had the shirt ripped off me!

That bloke's been trying to nail me
all match, so every time he has a go
I hold out my arms all innocent, like.

Watch out – here comes the cross!
That midfielder came out of nowhere!
It's in the net. We're dead and buried now!

Oh my back! I can't move. Carrying that
centre forward all game has done me in.
They're going to stretcher me off.

The St. John's Ambulance man is wiping my face
with the magic sponge. I'm crossing over
the white line. I'm going down into the tunnel.

OFF-THE-BALL INCIDENTS

Sometimes the winter snow engulfed the town.
A hundred fans with shovels cleared the field.
A legend died, the country mourned his death.
One silent minute thousands held their breath.

One time, a small black dog ran on the pitch.
Another time a bird perched on the bar.
A teenage lad had several slashes stitched.
A boy of nine had set fire to a car.

The tannoy called a name out at half time –
Some punter's new-born child was doing fine.
One spectator slipped and wrenched his spine.
The programme notes extolled the season's climb.

And of all that the radio said this –
A non-event, a bore: a no-score draw.

LOOK AWAY NOW

If you don't want to know the score:

The Linesman's flagging, and so is your team.
A figure in black is haunting your dreams.

He's judge and jury of who is at fault.
The season will turn on this one result.

The banners are sagging, the chanting has stopped.
Your wife's disappeared while out at the shops.

A note on the table, a valediction,
a wedding ring pinned to the inscription.

The girl from your office has spilled the beans
to your wife on the phone, a bitter scene.

Your son's away with friends out the back
giving him needle, they're having the crack.

Your doctor's report is crossing his desk,
affirming results from your screening test.

A penalty's given. A minute to go.
Look away now if you don't want to know.

THE SWEET SILVER SONG
(I.M. Ted Gibbons (1927-2003)

Rita, Keith and I are in the British Legion
to choose a menu for the wake.

We're at the end of the long bar.
It's early afternoon and the Staff are busily
taking stock to the sound of music
piped through speakers.

Rita points to the far end of the bar –

Dad's photo is pinned to the Obituary board
if you want to take a look.

I know it's the one where he's sitting at a table
wearing his green Liverpool away shirt.
He's grinning, offering a pint to the camera

The instant I stand in front of the photo,
smiling back at him, a shower of silver words
rain from the speaker above my head:

When you walk through a storm,
hold your head up high
and don't be afraid of the dark,
at the end of the storm there's a golden sky
and the sweet silver song of the lark. . .

This tune, our bonding song down all the seasons,
gives me my life's one holy moment,
washing away my grief.

I stand in baffled silence, innocent as an infant,
reunited with my father until the last note fades.

I walk on, a sinner
ambushed by angels.

Eddie Gibbons' two previous collections of
poetry, *Stations of the Heart* and *The Republic
of Ted* were published by Thirsty Books.

He has given readings in Berlin by invitation of
The British Council,
at the Edinburgh Fringe Festival,
the Auslandsgesellschaft, Dortmund,
at the Bloomsbury Theatre, London,
the Aberdeen Wordfringe Festival,
the Aberdeen WORD Festival,
The Poetry Café, London, and the
Cornelia Street Café, New York.

His footballing career was sadly terminated
when his Youth Club team manager dropped
him on the eve of his only local Cup Final.
He's been sulking ever since.